Burnley Foo
Quiz Book

101 Questions To Test Your Knowledge Of Burnley FC

Published by Glowworm Press
7 Nuffield Way
Abingdon OX14 1RL

By Chris Carpenter

Burnley FC

This book contains one hundred and one informative and entertaining trivia questions with multiple choice answers. Some questions are easy, some less so and all in all it is a good mix of questions for Burnley fans young and not so young. This entertaining book will test your knowledge and memory of the club's long and successful history.

You will be asked questions on a wide range of topics associated with **Burnley FC** for you to test yourself. You will be quizzed on players, legends, managers, opponents, transfer deals, trophies, records, honours, fixtures, songs and more guaranteeing you both an educational and fun experience. This Burnley Football Club Quiz Book will provide the ultimate in entertainment for fans of all ages and will test your knowledge of Burnley Football Club.

2023/24 Season Edition

FOREWORD

When I was asked to write a foreword to this book I was deeply honoured.

I have known the author Chris Carpenter for many years and his knowledge of facts and figures is phenomenal.

His love for football and his talent for writing quiz books makes him the ideal man to pay homage to my great love Burnley Football Club.

This book came about as a result of a challenge in a Lebanese restaurant of all places!

I do hope you enjoy the book.

Colin Dobson

Let's start with some relatively easy questions.

1. When were Burnley founded?
   A. 1881
   B. 1882
   C. 1883

2. What is Burnley's nickname?
   A. The Potters
   B. The Warriors
   C. The Clarets

3. Where does Burnley play their home games?
   A. Ewood Park
   B. Rose Bowl
   C. Turf Moor

4. What is the stadium's capacity?
   A. 21,344
   B. 21,644
   C. 21,944

5. Who or what is the club mascot?
   A. Boris Bee
   B. Bobby Bee
   C. Bertie Bee

6. Who has made the most appearances for the club in total?
   A. George Beel
   B. Jerry Dawson
   C. Jimmy McIlroy

7. Who has made the most appearances for the club in the post-war era?
   A. John Angus
   B. Jimmy McIlroy
   C. Alan Stevenson

8. Who is the club's record goal scorer?
   A. George Beel
   B. Jimmy McIlroy
   C. Andy Payton

9. How many goals did he score for the club?
   A. 168
   B. 178
   C. 188

10. Which of these is a well-known pub near the ground?
    A. The Beehive
    B. The Parrot
    C. The Turf

OK, so here are the answers to the first ten questions. Be warned though, the questions do get harder.

A1. Burnley FC were founded way back in 1882, and they played their first competitive game in October of that year.

A2. Burnley are nicknamed The Clarets due to the dominant colour of their famous claret and blue kit.

A3. Burnley plays their home games at Turf Moor, which has been home to the club since 1883.

A4. Turf Moor currently has a maximum capacity of 21,944.

A5. Bertie Bee is of course the club's mascot.

A6. Jerry Dawson has made the most appearances for the club with an astounding 569 appearances in total from 1907 to 1929.

A7. Goalkeeper Alan Stevenson has made the most appearances for the club since the war. He made a grand total of 543 appearances for the club between 1972 and 1983. Legend.

A8. Centre forward George Beel is the club's record goal scorer.

A9. Beel scored an impressive 188 goals for the club in his time at the club (including 179 in the League) between 1929 and 1932.

A10. The Turf is the place to go to have a quick one before the game. Be prepared to queue for a pint though.

OK, back to the questions.

11. What is the highest number of points that Burnley have recorded in a league season?
    A. 91
    B. 95
    C. 101

12. During which season did the club achieve the highest number of points in a season?
    A. 2011/12
    B. 2013/14
    C. 2015/16

13. In what League did they achieve the highest number of points recorded in a season?
    A. Championship
    B. Division 2
    C. Division 3

14. What song do the players run out to?
    A. Wake Up
    B. Just Lose It
    C. We Will Rock You

15. What are the hard-core home supporters known as?
    A. Bravehearts
    B. Burnley Brawlers
    C. Suicide Squad

16. What is the club's record attendance?

A. 54,775
B. 55,775
C. 56,775

17. Where is Burnley's training ground?
    A. Gawthorpe Hall
    B. Lancashire Manor
    C. Leck Hall

18. What is the name of the road the ground is on?
    A. James Hargreaves Road
    B. Harry Potts Road
    C. Yorkshire Street

19. Which stand has the biggest capacity?
    A. David Fishwick Stand
    B. James Hargreaves Stand
    C. Bob Lord Stand

20. What is the size of the pitch?
    A. 114 x 72 yards
    B. 115 x 75 yards
    C. 116 x 73 yards

OK, so here are the answers to the last set of questions.

A11. The highest amount of points Burnley have recorded in a season is 101.

A12. The record number of points came in the incredible 2022/23 season. This total surpassed the previous record of 93 points achieved in both the 2013/14 and 2015/16 seasons.

A13. This record points total was achieved in the Championship, resulting in automatic promotion to the Premier League.

A14. The players run out to the song "Wake Up" recorded by Arcade Fire.

A15. Suicide Squad is the name given to the hard core group of Burnley supporters.

A16. The club's highest ever attendance is 54,775 against Huddersfield Town in the 3rd round of the FA Cup on 23rd February 1924.

A17. Burnley's training ground is located at Gawthorpe Hall, near Padiham.

A18. The ground is located on Harry Potts Road, named in honour of the 1958 to 1970 manager.

A19. The James Hargreaves Stand has the largest capacity, being able to accommodate over 8,000 spectators.

A20. The pitch is 114 yards long x 72 yards wide.

Now we move onto some questions about the club's records.

21. What is the club's record win in a cup competition?
    A. 9-0
    B. 10-0
    C. 11-0

22. Who did they beat?
    A. Crystal Palace
    B. New Brighton
    C. Penrith

23. What is the club's record win in the League?
    A. 7-0
    B. 8-0
    C. 9-0

24. Who did they beat?
    A. Blackburn
    B. Darwen
    C. Preston North End

25. In which season?
    A. 1890/91
    B. 1891/92
    C. 1892/93

26. What is the club's record defeat?
    A. 0-10
    B. 0-11

C. 0-12

27. Who against?
    A. Aston Villa
    B. Darwen
    C. Penrith

28. In which season?
    A. 1883/84
    B. 1884/85
    C. 1885/86

29. Who has scored the most hat tricks for Burnley?
    A. George Beel
    B. Willie Irvine
    C. Louis Page

30. Who started the 2023/24 season as goalkeeping coach?
    A. Tony Loughlan
    B. Billy Mercer
    C. Jelle ten Rouwelaar

Here are the answers to the last set of questions.

A21. Burnley's record cup victory is 9-0.

A22. Burnley have beaten three sides 9-0 in the FA Cup, so give yourself a bonus point if you knew that. Burnley beat Crystal Palace 9-0 on 10th February 1909 and New Brighton on 26th January 1957 and Penrith on 17th September 1984.

A23. Burnley's record win in the league was also a 9-0 stuffing.

A24. Burnley cruised to a 9-0 victory against Darwen.

A25. The club's victory was on 9th January 1892; thus it was in the 1891/92 season.

A26. Burnley's biggest defeat is an 11-0 loss, sustained in an FA Cup tie.

A27. This massive defeat came against Darwen when eligibility restrictions meant that Burnley had to field a reserve side.

A28. Burnley lost 11-0 to Darwen in the first round of the FA Cup on 17th October 1885, during the 1885/86 season.

A29. George Beel has scored the most hat tricks for Burnley; he scored a total of 10 in his Burnley career.

A30. Jelle ten Rouwelaar started the 2023/24 season as goalkeeping coach.

Now we move onto some questions about the club's trophies.

31. How many times have Burnley won the top League title?
   A. 1
   B. 2
   C. 3

32. How many times have Burnley won the FA Cup?
   A. 1
   B. 2
   C. 3

33. How many times have the club won the Community Shield?
   A. 0
   B. 1
   C. 2

34. When did the club win their first league title?
   A. 1910/11
   B. 1920/21
   C. 1930/31

35. When did the club win their first FA Cup?
   A. 1914
   B. 1924
   C. 1934

36. Who did they beat in the final?

A. Aston Villa
B. Liverpool
C. Wimbledon

37. What was the score?
    A. 1-0
    B. 2-0
    C. 2-1

38. Who scored the winning goal?
    A. Bert Freeman
    B. Eddie Mosscrop
    C. Billy Nesbit

39. Who was the last captain to lift the League trophy?
    A. Tommy Boyle
    B. Steven Caldwell
    C. John Pender

40. Who was the last captain to lift the FA Cup?
    A. Tommy Boyle
    B. Steven Caldwell
    C. John Pender

Here is the latest set of answers.

A31. Burnley have won the League twice, in 1920/21 and 1959/60. Incidentally they are one of just three teams to have won the title in all of England's top tier leagues.

A32. Burnley have won the FA Cup just once; in 1914.

A33. Burnley have won the Community Shield twice; in 1960 and 1973.

A34. The club won their first league title way back in the 1920/21 season.

A35. Burnley won the FA Cup in 1914.

A36. Burnley beat Liverpool in the 1914 FA Cup Final, held at Crystal Palace.

A37. Burnley beat Liverpool 1-0 in the FA Cup Final on 25th April 1914.

A38. Bert Freeman scored the only goal of the game in the 57th minute to win Burnley the FA Cup.

A39. John Pender was the last captain to lift the league trophy for Burnley.

A40. Tommy Boyle is the only captain who has lifted the FA Cup for the club.

I hope you're getting most of the answers right.

41. What is the record transfer fee paid?
    A. £14.1 million
    B. £15.1 million
    C. £16.1 million

42. Who was the record transfer fee paid for?
    A. Zeki Amdouni
    B. Ben Gibson
    C. Chris Wood

43. What is the record transfer fee received?
    A. £23 million
    B. £25 million
    C. £27 million

44. Who was the record transfer fee received for?
    A. Andre Gray
    B. Michael Keane
    C. Chris Wood

45. Who was the first Burnley player to play for England?
    A. Bert Freeman
    B. Bob Kelly
    C. Jack Yates

46. Who has won the most international caps whilst a Burnley player?
    A. Brian Flynn

B. Bert Freeman
C. Jimmy McIlroy

47. Who has scored the most international goals whilst a Burnley player?
    A. Willie Irvine
    B. Leighton James
    C. Jimmy McIlroy

48. Who is the youngest player ever to represent the club?
    A. George Beel
    B. Alex Elder
    C. Tommy Lawton

49. Who is the youngest ever goalscorer?
    A. George Beel
    B. Tommy Lawton
    C. Ray Pointer

50. Who is the oldest player ever to represent the club?
    A. Jimmy Adamson
    B. Jerry Dawson
    C. Alan Stevenson

Here are the answers to the last set of questions.

A41. The record transfer fee paid by the club is £16.1 million.

A42. This record fee was paid to FC Basel for midfielder Zeki Amdouni in July 2023.

A43. The record fee the club has received is £27 million.

A44. £27 million was received for Chris Wood in January 2022 when he moved to Newcastle United. It beat the previous record of £25.6 million which was received for Michael Keane in July 2017 when he moved to Everton.

A45. Jack Yates was the first Burnley player to play for England; he made his debut against Ireland in June 1889.

A46. Jimmy McIlroy won 51 caps for Northern Ireland whilst a Burnley player, the most international caps any Burnley player has won.

A47. Jimmy McIlroy also scored the most international goals whilst a Burnley player, scoring 10 goals in his 51 appearances for his country.

A48. Tommy Lawton is the youngest player to represent the club; he made his first appearance on

28th March 1936 against Doncaster Rovers aged just 16 years and 163 days.

A49. Tommy Lawton became the club's youngest ever goal scorer when he scored in his second game for the club aged just 16 years and 170 days at Swansea Town (yes, they used to be called that) on 4th April 1936.

A50. Goalkeeper Jerry Dawson is the oldest player to represent the club; he was 40 years and 282 days when he played his final game for the club in 1928.

I hope you're having fun and learning some new facts about the Clarets.

51. Who is the club's longest serving manager of all time?
    A. John Haworth
    B. Brian Miller
    C. Harry Potts

52. How long did he serve as manager?
    A. 10 years
    B. 12 years
    C. 14 years

53. Who is the club's longest serving post-war manager?
    A. Brian Miller
    B. Harry Potts
    C. Stan Ternent

54. How long did he serve as manager of the club?
    A. 10 years
    B. 12 years
    C. 14 years

55. What is the name of the Burnley match day programme?
    A. Beekeepers
    B. Turf
    C. Turf More

56. Which of these is a popular unofficial website?
    A. Beekeepers
    B. Clarets Crazy
    C. Up The Clarets

57. What animal is on the club crest?
    A. Bee
    B. Canary
    C. Tiger

58. Who was the club's first non-English manager?
    A. John Benson
    B. Billy Dougall
    C. Frank Hill

59. Who is considered as Burnley's main rivals?
    A. Blackburn Rovers
    B. Preston North End
    C. Sheffield United

60. What could be regarded as the club's most well-known song?
    A. The Burnley Aces
    B. The Claret and Blues
    C. Don't Stop Believing

Here are the answers to the last block of questions.

A51. John Haworth is the club's longest serving manager of all time.

A52. John Haworth was at the helm of the club for 14 years from July 1910 to December 1924. He actually died whilst in office.

A53. Harry Potts is the club's longest serving post war manager.

A54. Potts served as manager of the club twice. The first spell was from 1958 to 1970, and he returned from 1977 to 1979.

A55. Turf is the name of the club's Matchday programme.

A56. Up the Clarets is a popular unofficial Burnley website.

A57. A bee is on the club's crest.

A58. Burnley had a long succession of English managers until 1948 when Scottish born manager Billy Dougall took over at the helm of the club.

A59. Blackburn Rovers are considered Burnley's main rivals.

A60. 'The Burnley Aces' is probably Burnley's most well-known song.

Let's give you some easier questions.

61. What is the traditional colour of the home shirt?
     A. Aquamarine and Blue
     B. Claret and Blue
     C. Green and Blue

62. What is the traditional colour of the away shirt?
     A. Blue
     B. White
     C. Yellow

63. Who is the current official shirt sponsor?
     A. Dafabet
     B. EMA Equity Partners
     C. W88

64. Who was the first shirt sponsor?
     A. Multipart
     B. P3 Computers
     C. Poco

65. Which of these banks have once sponsored the club?
     A. Halifax
     B. Lloyds
     C. TSB

66. Who is the club's current chairman?
     A. Mike Garlick

B. Stuart Hunt
C. Alan Pace

67. Who was the club's first foreign signing?
   A. Ade Akinbiyi
   B. Hanz Gruber
   C. Max Seeburg

68. Who was the club's first ever black player?
   A. Mo Camara
   B. Micah Evans
   C. Les Lawrence

69. Who was the club's first match against?
   A. Artley Bridge
   B. Hebden Bridge
   C. Stamford Bridge

70. Who was the supporters' player of the year
   for the 2022/23 season?
   A. Jack Cork
   B. Josh Brownhill
   C. Josh Cullen

Here are the answers to the last set of questions.

A61. Claret and Blue are Burnley's traditional home colours.

A62. Burnley's away kit is traditionally white.

A63. Gambling company W88 are the club's current shirt sponsor.

A64. The club was first sponsored by Poco, back in 1982.

A65. TSB has been the only bank to sponsor the club.

A66. Alan Pace is the current club chairman, following the takeover of the club in December 2020.

A67. Max Seeburg was the club's first foreign signing. This German defender was signed back in 1910 by manager John Haworth.

A68. Les Lawrence was Burnley's first ever black player. He signed for the club in 1984.

A69. Burnley's first ever competitive game came against Artley Bridge in October 1882 in the Lancashire Challenge Cup.

A70. Josh Cullen was voted the club's player of the year for the 2022/23 season. It was well deserved too.

71. On how many separate occasions did Leighton James join the club?
     A. 2
     B. 3
     C. 4

72. Which manager got Burnley promoted to the Premier League at the end of the 2008/09 season?
     A. Steve Cotterill
     B. Owen Coyle
     C. Eddie Howe

73. Who did Burnley beat in the 2009 Championship play-off final?
     A. Fulham
     B. Reading
     C. Sheffield United

74. Who scored the winning goal?
     A. Wade Elliot
     B. Martin Paterson
     C. Steven Thompson

75. What was the original name of Burnley FC?
     A. Burnley Rivers
     B. Burnley Rovers
     C. Burnley Town

76. Where did Burnley play before Turf Moor?
     A. Calder Park
     B. Calder Pit

C. Calder Vale

77. What position did the club finish at the end of the 2022/23 season?
    A. 1st
    B. 3rd
    C. 5th

78. From which club did Burnley sign Paul Gascoigne?
    A. Aston Villa
    B. Everton
    C. Tottenham Hotspur

79. Who started the 2023/24 season as manager?
    A. Sean Dyche
    B. Mike Jackson
    C. Vincent Kompany

80. Who started the 2023/24 season as captain?
    A. Jack Cork
    B. Connor Roberts
    C. Charlie Taylor

Here are the answers to the last block of questions.

A71. Leighton James signed for the club on 3 separate occasions.

A72. Owen Coyle managed to get Burnley into the Premier League at the end of the 2008/09 season.

A73. Burnley beat Sheffield United in the 2009 Championship play-off final.

A74. Burnley won the play-off final 1-0, with midfielder Wade Elliot scoring the only goal in front of 80,518 people at Wembley Stadium.

A75. Hard to believe but Burnley were originally known as Burnley Rovers.

A76. Burnley originally played their home games at Calder Vale before moving to Turf Moor in the early months of 1883.

A77. Burnley finished the 2022/23 top of the Championship, playing some great football too. What a truly memorable season it was.

A78. Gazza signed for Burnley on a free transfer from Everton back in May 2002.

A79. Vincent Kompany started the 2023/24 season as manager. He took office in June 2022.

A80. Jack Cork started the 2023/24 season as captain.

Here's the next block of questions.

81. Who was the last Burnley player to win a full
England cap?
- A. Ralph Coates
- B. Martin Dobson
- C. Steve Davis

82. How many times has Steve Davis been
caretaker manager?
- A. 1
- B. 2
- C. 3

83. Which team did Burnley copy when
designing their kit?
- A. Aston Villa
- B. Scunthorpe United
- C. West Ham United

84. What is the club's official website?
- A. burnleyfootballclub.com
- B. burnleyfc.com
- C. turfmoor.com

85. Which of these politicians is a lifelong
supporter of Burnley?
- A. Tony Blair
- B. Alastair Campbell
- C. Alastair Darling

86. How many times has Andy Payton won the player of the season award?
    A. 1
    B. 2
    C. 3

87. Who is the current Burnley kit supplier?
    A. Errea
    B. Puma
    C. Umbro

88. From which club did Burnley sign Jack Cork from?
    A. Stoke City
    B. Swansea City
    C. Swindon Town

89. Which member of the Royal Family is an avid Burnley fan?
    A. King Charles
    B. Prince Harry
    C. Prince William

90. Who joined Bertie Bee as the club's mascot during the 2006/07 season?
    A. Peter the Pukka Pie
    B. Pie Face
    C. Stan the Pie Man

Here is the latest set of answers.

A81. Martin Dobson was the last Burnley player to earn a full England cap.

A82. Steve Davis has been Burnley's caretaker manager twice.

A83. Burnley took their inspiration for their claret and blue kit from Aston Villa.

A84. The club's official website is burnleyfootballclub.com.

A85. Alastair Campbell is an avid Burnley supporter.

A86. The Padiham Predator Andy Payton won the player of the year award three times during his five seasons at the club between 1998 and 2003.

A87. As from the 2019/20 season, Umbro is the current official kit supplier.

A88. Jack Cork joined from Swansea City in July 2017.

A89. King Charles is a loyal Burnley supporter.

A90. Burnley brought in a new mascot for the 2006/07 season due to a sponsorship deal with Holland's Pies. The new mascot was called Stan the Pie Man.

Here is the last set of questions.

91. In 1886, Turf Moor became the first ground to do what?
    A. Let ladies in for free
    B. Sell hot dogs outside the ground
    C. Be visited by the Royal Family

92. Where was Johan Berg Gudmundsson born?
    A. Iceland
    B. Norway
    C. Sweden

93. What shirt number does Charlie Taylor wear?
    A. 3
    B. 13
    C. 23

94. Who holds the club's record as top league scorer, but with the fewest number of goals?
    A. Steven Fletcher
    B. Louis Page
    C. Eric Probert

95. Who holds the club's record for most goals scored in a game?
    A. George Beel
    B. Ray Pointer
    C. Louis Page

96. Which of these brands has not supplied Burnley with their kit?

A. Adidas
B. Nike
C. Puma

97. Which of these is not a nickname for the club?
   A. The Clarets
   B. The Dingles
   C. The Rovers

98. During which season did Burnley compete in the European Cup?
   A. 1959/60
   B. 1960/61
   C. 1961/62

99. What is the club's official twitter account?
   A. @burnley
   B. @burnleyfc
   C. @burnleyofficial

100. Which famous ex-chairman has a stand named after him at Turf Moor?
   A. Bob Geldof
   B. Bob Lord
   C. Bob Maxwell

101. What is the club's motto?
   A. Heart of a lion
   B. Hold to the truth
   C. Keep moving forward

Here is the final set of answers.

A91. On 13 October 1886, Prince Albert visited Turf Moor which thus became the first ground to be visited by a member of the British Royal Family.

A92. Gudmundsson was born in Reykjavik in Iceland.

A93. Left back Taylor wears shirt number 3.

A94. Eric Probert holds the record for being the club's top goal scorer for a season with the fewest number of goals scored. Probert managed to score 5 goals during the 1969/70 season, but he was still the club's top goal scorer that season.

A95. Louis Page holds the record for the most goals scored in a single game, scoring six goals in the 7-1 victory over Birmingham City on 10 April 1926.

A96. Nike has never been the kit supplier for Burnley.

A97. Burnley have never had the Rovers as their nickname.

A98. Burnley competed in the European Cup during the 1960/61 season, eventually losing out to German side Hamburger SV in the quarter finals.

A99. @BurnleyOfficial is the club's official twitter account. It tweets multiple times daily and has almost a million followers.

A100. The epitome of autocracy and a ruler with an iron fist, Bob Lord was chairman from 1955 until 1981. The stand that was named after him was built in 1974, and was opened by Edward Heath, the Conservative Party leader at the time.

A101. The official club motto is "Hold to the truth."

That's it. That's a great question to finish with. I hope you enjoyed this book, and I hope you got most of the answers right, and I hope you learnt some new facts about the club.

support@glowwormpress.com is the email address if you saw anything wrong, or you have any comments or suggestions.

Thanks for reading, and if you did enjoy the book, would you please leave a positive review on Amazon.

Printed in Great Britain
by Amazon

33245032R00025